Atheneum

ATHENEUM BOOKS FOR YOUNG READERS

An imprint of Simon & Schuster Children's Publishing Division

1230 Avenue of the Americas, New York, New York 10020

ATHENEUM BOOKS FOR YOUNG READERS is a registered trademark of
Simon & Schuster, Inc.

Atheneum logo is a trademark of Simon & Schuster, Inc.

For information about special discounts for bulk purchases,
please contact Simon & Schuster Special Sales at 1-866-506-1949
or business@simonandschuster.com.

The Simon & Schuster Speakers Bureau can bring authors to your live
event. For more information or to book an event, contact the Simon &
Schuster Speakers Bureau at 1-866-248-3049 or visit our website at
www.simonspeakers.com.

Book design by Sonia Chaghatzbanian

The text for this book is set in Raleigh LT Std.

The illustrations for this book are rendered in watercolor.

Manufactured in China

0614 SCP

First Edition

10 9 8 7 6 5 4 3 2 1

Library of Congress Cataloging-in-Publication Data

Winter, Jonah, 1962-

Joltin' Joe DiMaggio / Jonah Winter ; illustrated by James E. Ransome.

p. cm

Summary: "The baseball legend, Joe DiMaggio's picture book
biography"—Provided by publisher.

Includes bibliographical references and index.

ISBN 978-1-4169-4080-7 (hc.)—ISBN 978-1-4814-0279-8 (eBook)

1. DiMaggio, Joe, 1914-1999—Juvenile literature. 2. Baseball players—
United States—Biography—Juvenile literature. I. Ransome, James, ill.
II. Title.

GV865.D5W55 2014

796.357092—dc23

[B]

2014009584

Joltin' Joe DiMaggio

Jonah Winter

Illustrated by
James E. Ransome

ATHENEUM BOOKS FOR YOUNG READERS
New York London Toronto Sydney New Delhi

For my mother-in-law, Maria Denmead, who is also my favorite Italian-American.
—J. W.

For my father-in-law, William "Bill" Cline, who has always treated me like a son.
—J. E. R.

Baseball, believe it or not, was once the biggest sport in America—bigger than football, bigger than basketball. And it wasn't just the biggest sport—it was the *biggest thing*.

Back in the roaring 1920s, baseball was all people talked about for seven months out of the year. Would the New York Yankees win the pennant again? Did Babe Ruth hit a homer today? How many bases did Ty Cobb steal?

From New York
        to Detroit
                to Chicago, baseball *ruled*
the radio waves and the newspaper headlines. Even out west
in San Francisco, where they didn't have a major league team,
baseball was big news.

"READ ALL ABOUT IT!
READ ALL ABOUT IT!"

a newsboy shouted from a hill in San Francisco.

"YANKS WIN THE PENNANT!"

The newsboy was just a scrawny kid trying to make a couple of bucks. His name: Joe DiMaggio.

Like most American boys, Joe mainly cared about one thing: baseball.
Joe and his pals played baseball every day in the playground lot just up
the hill from Fisherman's Wharf.

Joe's dad was a fisherman from Italy, and he mainly cared about one thing too: fish. He expected all his sons to become fishermen just like him. But Joe hated boats, hated the smell of fish, and hated how hard his father worked for so little money. Joe would not become a fisherman, and that was that.

Joe came from a big, talkative family, and he thought maybe, if he just kept really quiet, no one would notice that he wasn't helping out on the boat.

And Joe thought maybe no one would notice that he had dropped out of school and was spending a lot of his free time playing baseball with his buddies.

But as Joe got bigger and taller from his mama's good cooking, it became hard not to notice him. He was quiet, he was shy, but the guy was six-foot-two! Joe got noticed all right . . .

. . . and not just by his family. As it turned out, Joe was pretty darn good at hitting a baseball. He was so good, in fact, that he got asked to play for the San Francisco Seals. They weren't a major league team, but they were good and they paid well. That is, they paid better than being a fisherman. Joe was only seventeen, and this was a good job. At least, he thought so.

Joe's father had other ideas.

"*É che cosa e questo . . .* 'baseball'?!?" Joe's dad shouted in Italian when he heard the news.

"In English, Dad," Joe said.

"It's not a job," Joe's dad said. "*Non é il lavoro. É il gioco! Sei uomo ora. Hai bisogno di lavorare.*" ("It's not work. It's play! You're a man now. You need to work.")

"Oh, don't be so hard on my Joe," Joe's mama said. "He's a good boy."

But Joe's dad was no dummy, and when he saw all the money
Joe brought in, he changed his tune. And when he started seeing
Joe's name in the paper every day, he got downright proud:
DIMAGGIO HITS SAFELY IN 42ND STRAIGHT GAME.
"Cio e il mio raguzzo!" Joe's father said to the other fishermen.
("That's my boy!") "This *'baseball'*—it's the most wonderful game!"
Joe, he kept his mouth shut and kept on swinging that bat,

game after game, hit after hit, until he had broken a record for his league. He had hit safely in sixty-one straight games. In San Francisco, Joe was famous. But when the reporters asked him questions, he never knew what to say. So he just smiled. Wasn't it enough that he was a good hitter? Why did he have to say anything?

The truth was, he didn't have to say a word. The way Joe swung a bat was good enough for San Francisco, and it was also good enough for the . . .

New York Yankees??? Uh-huh. That's right. When Joe was only nineteen, he got signed to America's *greatest team.* And that's not all—the Yankees agreed to pay him *twenty-five thousand* dollars.

That was a lot of money back then. The year was 1934, and America was in the middle of the Great Depression. Thousands and thousands of people were out of work, standing in unemployment lines.

As Joe drove across the country to spring training, he saw people living in shacks and shanties. He saw hoboes in ragged clothes without any homes at all. It was a sad sight.

But baseball! Now here was a thing that took everyone's minds off the Great Depression. And when Joe arrived at spring training in Florida, all the photographers were there, ready to snap some pictures of the new *star*.

TODAY'S lineup

Frank Crosetti
Red Rolfe
Joe DiMaggio
Lou Gehrig
Bill Dickey
Ben Chapman
George Selkirk
Tony Lazzeri
Lefty Gomez

You see, Babe Ruth, the greatest of all Yankee stars, was gone. He had just retired. Everybody knew that this DiMaggio kid was being brought in to fill Babe's shoes. And those were some pretty big shoes. Joe was terrified. What if he failed? Would he have to go work on a fishing boat?

Joe knew one thing, though—he wasn't going to let anyone see he was nervous. It was none of their business. In his first at-bat in Yankee pinstripes, with everyone watching to see what the new kid would do . . .

BABE RUTH

. . . Joe hit a weak grounder to third base, drove home a run, and wound up on second base: his first hit as a Yankee!

And so began Joe DiMaggio's life with the New York Yankees. It only got better. Overnight, Joe was the talk of the town. He was the new Babe Ruth. But not even the great Bambino himself had had such an amazing rookie year—29 homers, 125 RBIs, and a .323 batting average. In a New York minute Joe was plastered all over the papers.

With every sizzling hit, he made news.

With every graceful catch, he made news. No one had ever seen such a natural center fielder.

For Joe, this was scary. He was still just a kid.

And he still had no idea how to talk to reporters. But it didn't take him long to figure one thing out: The less he said, the more they wrote. All he had to do was keep his mouth shut and keep getting hits. And that he did, week in and week out.

And weeks turned into years . . .

. . . and Joe became "Joltin' Joe," a star with a nickname, a star who cheered people up. It was 1941. The Great Depression was over. But the world was at war, and America might have to enter that war. People were worried. Again, the papers were filled with bad news. Again, you had to turn to the sports pages for anything good. And there was a photo of Joe with that WIDE swing of his . . .

. . . *crushing* another ball into the stands, game after game after game, until he'd hit in thirty straight games and it was official: This was a hitting streak—maybe one for the record books. With each game he got a hit, Joltin' Joe got that much more quiet, slipping off into the dressing room when it was done. He didn't want to talk about it, didn't want to jinx it.

Even on the train rides between towns, Joe kept to himself.
His teammates treated him like a king, always making sure he had
everything he wanted.

"You want a cuppa coffee, Joe?"

"Nah, I'm okay."

"Only three hours left till we get to Philly."

"N'kay," Joe said, and that was about the most you'd get out of him.

After games, Joe's roommate, Lefty Gomez, would make sure the coast was clear outside the dressing room, then he'd take Joe out to some quiet restaurant, where no reporters would bother him. Even so, it was hard not to notice Joe DiMaggio—the way he dressed in those fancy suits, the way he smiled, the way his picture appeared in the paper every day. He was not only "Joltin' Joe"—he was now the "Yankee Clipper." He was the most popular baseball player in New York, in America, in the world. And the way he said nothing . . . only made him more noticeable.

By the time Joe was one game away from the American League record of a forty-one-game hitting streak, he had to take a separate train from the rest of the Yankees. It was the only way he could get away from the reporters.

It was a tense game. The Washington Senators had their ace knuckleballer, "Dutch" Leonard, on the mound. Joe's first time up in the second inning, he popped up to center field. The center fielder caught it.

Out.

His second time up, he popped up to the infield. The third baseman caught it.

Out.

The next time Joe came up to bat, the crowd was nervous. Would Joltin' Joe break the record?

Or would this be the end? Before every pitch, the whole stadium got quiet.

First pitch, he swung and missed. Strike one.

Second pitch—low and inside. Ball one.

If Dutch Leonard could get Joe to swing at and miss one more pitch, he knew he'd have the edge. The third pitch was low and outside . . .

. . . and smacked by Joe into left center field, where it fell to the ground. Fair ball! Joe had tied the American League hitting streak record that Geoge Sisler had set in 1922. The game stopped. The Washington fans cheered like crazy. They didn't care if Joe was on the Yankees. They had just seen history being made.

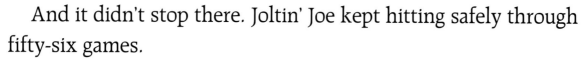

   And it didn't stop there. Joltin' Joe kept hitting safely through fifty-six games.
   By the fifty-seventh game, when he finally went hitless, he was larger than life. He was a hundred feet tall, and he was holding America in the palms of his hands, right there next to the Statue of Liberty.

If you turned on the radio, you could hear this song:

He'll live in baseball's Hall of Fame.
He got there blow by blow.
Our kids will tell their kids his name:
Joltin' Joe DiMaggio.

America was different back then. A baseball player could become more famous than a movie star. A baseball player could become the symbol of everything good about America.

A baseball player could go on to marry Marilyn Monroe, the most glamorous actress of all time. Well, there was one baseball player who could.

He was born with the name of
Giuseppe Paolo DiMaggio Jr. in an age
when Italian Americans endured fierce
prejudice. Years later he showed the
world that you could go from being
a scrawny kid selling papers on the
corner, the son of an Italian fisherman,
to becoming the country's most
beloved star. It's called the American
Dream, and Joe DiMaggio was one of
the greatest dreams America ever had.
If you close your eyes, you can still
hear the fans roar as Joltin' Joe knocks
another one into the bleachers, a
hitting streak that won't ever end,
just can't ever end. . . .

Author's Note & Stats

Joe DiMaggio, the son of Italian immigrants, was in fact born with the name

Giuseppe Paolo DiMaggio Jr. in Martinez, California on November 25, 1914. When people speak of the "greatest baseball players of all time," the ones almost everyone has heard of, they generally start with the three most famous New York Yankees: Babe Ruth, Lou Gehrig, and Joe DiMaggio. DiMaggio's classic, graceful fielding is still considered by many to be the greatest of all time. And his powerful hitting and wide stance at the plate were things to behold. But as this story suggests, DiMaggio was more than just a great baseball player—he was like a movie star! And what his star power did for the acceptance of Italian Americans into mainstream American culture cannot be measured. Famous for being reserved and dignified, the "Yankee Clipper" wasn't very talkative. When people now speak of what a "class act" he was, they are referring in part to the fact he let his baseball skills do the talking. He didn't boast, didn't throw temper tantrums, and didn't talk to reporters much. This, of course, only added to his mystique. For many Americans, he came to symbolize the golden era of baseball. Even in the 1960s, long after he had retired, his name wound up in a very popular song by Paul Simon: *Where have you gone, Joe DiMaggio? Our nation turns its lonely eyes to you.* DiMaggio was somewhat confused by the song, since he figured that he hadn't gone anywhere! What definitely hasn't gone anywhere . . . is DiMaggio's 56-game hitting streak, which many sports fans consider to be the most unbreakable record and the most magnificent accomplishment in the history of sports. His other lifetime statistics, though impressive, simply do not tell the whole story of his greatness. Like so many ballplayers of his era, he lost crucial years (and stats) while serving three years in the US Armed Forces during World War II. On the other hand, his military service only added to his legendary aura. As for his famous, though brief, marriage to Marilyn Monroe, his legendary status continued to grow with every half-dozen roses he placed on her grave after she had died—three times a week, for twenty years. Joltin' Joe died on March 8, 1999. He is missed.

DiMaggio's lifetime hitting stats, amassed during his 13-year career with the NY Yankees (from 1936 to 1951, excluding his three years of military service, 1943–45):

Batting Avg.	Runs	Hits	Doubles	Triples	Home Runs	Runs Batted In
.325	1,390	2,214	389	131	361	1,537

Awards:

3 Most Valuable Player Awards (1939, 1941, 1947)
Associated Press Athlete of the Year in 1941
9 World Championships
10 American League Pennants
11 All-Star Games
Major League Baseball Hall of Fame induction in 1955
Major League Baseball All-Century Team inclusion in 1999